WHAT, WHY, AND HOW?

-2-

Aslı Kaplan

New Jersey

15 14 13 12 1 2 3 4

Originally published in Turkish as *Ne, Niçin, Nasıl?-2* in 2006.

Published by Tughra Books
345 Clifton Ave., Clifton,
NJ, 07011, USA

www.tughrabooks.com

Library of Congress Cataloging-in-Publication Data Available

Translated by Mustafa Mencütekin

ISBN: 978-1-59784-287-7

Printed by
Çağlayan A.Ş., Izmir - Turkey

Contents

Preface

Let us suppose this universe is a book waiting to be read. Let's flip through its pages together. What do you see? Look to the right, look at the countless beauties displayed to you in the most beautiful and flawless manner. Look to the left, look at the artistry in each blessing and how each is a distinct wonder of creation. Don't close the book just yet...

The universe is a book showing its Maker, the All-Manifesting, the All-Sublime and the All-Wise Maker, and the manifestation of His Divine names and attributes. There are certain aims and wisdom in the creation of all living and non-living beings in this book and our prime obligation as readers are to understand, appreciate and act in conformity with them.

As readers of the book of the universe, we need to first understand that the All-Favoring and All-Bountiful creates all the beauty and art that surrounds us, regardless of whether we are aware or unaware of it. We need to then appreciate the All-Bestowing, Who constantly renews each of these blessings and continues displaying astonishing wonders in each page on the book of the universe with perfect artistry and wisdom.

The book of the universe is there for us to also recognize the Creator and to act in conformity with His wisdom. It is there for us to understand that we live with His will and permission, and to remind us that we will inevitably return to Him and be questioned about what we saw and experienced in this world and about the proofs showcased to us.

As the protagonists of this book, we can see that all living entities showcase countless proofs, perfections and wisdom in their creation. There is wisdom in the structure of a tiny particle, the building block of external existence. There is wisdom in the vast universe which has been being created with extraordinary balance and order. There is wisdom in the human body, plants and animals, the mountains and the seas. All of these wonders are the manifestations of the All-Wise and the All-Manifesting.

Our duty as readers, both of this book and the book of the universe, is simple: to recognize and thank the All-Praiseworthy One for all the unconditional beauties and bounties that He has bestowed upon us. Through scientific principles and fascinating facts, this book seeks to remind us of this important duty...

> "God it is Who has made the sea to be of service to you by making it subservient (to His command) so that the ships may run through it by His command, and that you may seek of His bounty, and that (in return) you may give thanks." (Al-Jathiyah, 45:12)

What is muscle fatigue?

Muscle fatigue can be defined as muscle weakness felt when muscles are forced or used for a long time, together with a kind of pain that comes from deep inside. In other words, it is the temporary imbalance between the muscle's capacity of producing energy and the energy needed. When energy need is more than the energy obtained, the feeling of fatigue causes a decrease in the particular work done by the muscle cell. At the end, the cell is protected from any kind of damage. Since energy is necessary for the mechanisms that provide liveliness of the cell, fatigue is a very beneficial protection mechanism, created by the All-Wise and the All-Merciful. If this feature had not been foreordained, we wouldn't leave working and would force our cells until they totally die. When fatigue occurs in a forced muscle, the muscle activity is totally left or the level of density is decreased. So, in every way, the probable damage is prevented in muscles, tendons, ligaments and bones. If there were no feeling of fatigue, since we can't know which muscle activities can damage the skeletal system, we would frequently experience breaking off on muscle fibers or bonds and bleeding inside our muscles.

What is molasses?

Molasses is a thick tempered fruit juice which is thickened by boiling and prevented from souring by fermentation. Molasses is generally made from grapes. Juicy fruit, the juice of which will be extracted to make molasses, is put in strained pots. These pots are left under pressure, and after a certain time its juice is extracted. After removing its pomace, it is boiled on a vivid fire. Marl, also known as "molasses soil," is added to temper the juicy liquid. So, your molasses is ready for consumption: a fruit juice which is rather thick and has a lot of sugar in it.

Is molasses really an "iron store"?

In case of deficiency of mineral substances, various growing distortions take place in our body. The most significant of them is the deficiency of the iron element which resides in the structure of hemoglobin and functions the transfer of oxygen through our blood. Bivalent iron is used for producing hemoglobin which is a molecule in charge of transferring the oxygen in blood. Besides, it works as an important regulator factor in bone marrow. Since our defense cells are created from bone marrow, any kind of defection there means that our body becomes defenseless. A separate process should be followed in the body in order to convert trivalent iron that is taken as tablets to bivalent iron. This converting process can't be realized in some situations like vitamin C deficiency. The iron in molasses is bivalent iron that human body can use very easily. If one's diet contains only molasses, he/she can meet 35% of his/her daily need of iron.

What would we do without joints?

There are in total 360 joints in the human body, approximately 270 are movable and semi-movable, the rest are immovable and created in a combined form. If we didn't have joints, a stable skeleton wouldn't provide any use to our lives that we would not even be able to drink water. In contrast, we can walk and do many activities by means of our joints. God Almighty has created our skeleton and muscles within an all-knowing wisdom, suitable for certain purposes. All our joints have been endowed with the capability to move easily up to a particular angle so that our bones and muscles are able to move together with completeness and integration. If necessary attention is paid, it shall be observed that our daily activities are performed according to the limitations of our joints. For example, while wearing a cardigan, we can take our arms only 40 degrees back from our shoulders. While picking fruit from a tree, we can raise our arms as much as 170 degrees. We can raise our arms to our head with an angle of 180 degree. If these limitations on our joints did not exist, our shoulders would frequently dislocate. We wouldn't be able to take a heavy stone from the ground, wash our head, and clean our neck and back, get dressed easily without the supporting strength of our shoulders.

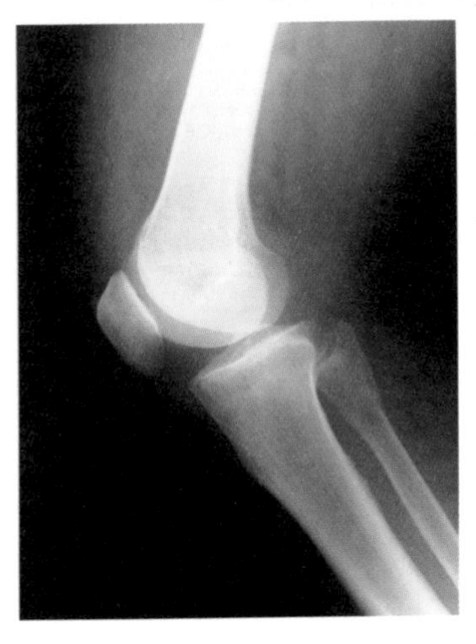

Why doesn't snow on high mountains melt away in summer?

Going up on mountains, the temperature decreases generally 1 degree Celsius every 180 meters. Likewise, as height increases, snow and its amount increases, as well. The snow on the summit of mountains does not melt during the summer and winter simply because the temperature on high parts at nights decreases below zero, even in the summer. Even though the weather is warmer during day time, the snow starting to melt freezes again due to the decreasing temperature. In some countries, never-melting snow is seen approximately after the altitude of 2700 meters.

What does the mother's milk contain?

The breast milk, which is also defined as an organic liquid, contains the nourishing elements necessary for the growth of baby, particularly protective substances against diseases and special materials empowering the immune system. Basic fat acids in the breast milk necessary for brain and nerve tissue are 8 times more than those in cow milk. The absorption rate of minerals—e.g. iron, zinc—through intestines that are necessary for growth and development of the baby is higher in the breast milk compared to the rate in cow milk and infant formula. The amount of cholesterol in breast milk is especially important in the first months to stimulate the development of enzyme systems and prevent the occurrence of arteriosclerosis in following ages. In short, the breast milk that has a vital importance for the baby does not only feed the baby but also makes a perfect bond between the baby and the mother, as a sign of God's absolute compassion.

What is jet-lag actually?

We have an internal biological clock that controls the operation order of our body. This inner clock which works according to certain time sections is influenced by external factors such as light and heat. Think about flying from İstanbul to New York. At that time, your biological clock is adjusted to the local time of İstanbul. Imagine that your plane takes off from İstanbul at 2:00 p.m. and when you arrive to New York after an 8-hour flight, your body clock is at 22:00 p.m. However, according to the local time, it is 15:00 p.m. at New York and your body clock is 7 hours fast. You will get hungry and after a time you will feel sleepy but there are 7-8 hours to the evening at that city. This event is called a "jet-lag." The English translation of the word "lag" is staying behind and delaying. In this situation, the person suffering from jet-lag feels extremely tired after the flight. Especially, lack of motivation and concentration is seen during activities such as reading, driving and job meetings.

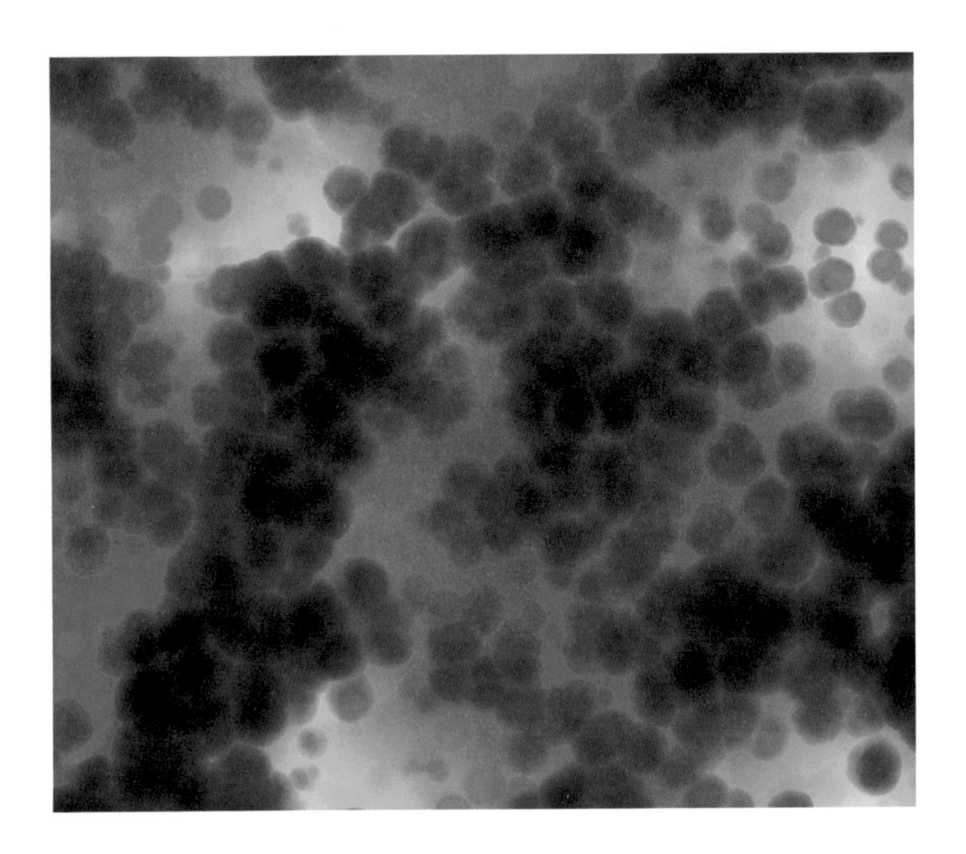

What does a beneficial bacterium mean?

Beneficial bacteria work in our body as soldiers in charge. Particular bacteria exist in urethra and reproduction canals, in our skin, throat, intestine and eyes which don't cause any disease in normal conditions. These beneficial bacteria that are placed as guests into our body work for us and prevent harmful bacteria from settling in these places. And this is the reason why taking antibiotics haphazardly is very harmful. Antibiotics do not only kill harmful bacteria but also the beneficial bacteria in our body.

What is nacre?

When dust, sand, pebble and harmful parasites go inside of mussels and oysters, these living beings are disturbed from this situation. They try to protect themselves from these foreign substances. So, they start to secrete a special substance from protector layer that covers their internal organs. This special secretion is called nacre or mother of pearl.

Are owls "flying radar stations"?

Under normal conditions it is not possible to hear the sound waves of a mouse eating a hazelnut in a hayloft. Possessing a sensitive receiver, owls are an exception. The facial structure of owls resembles the high tech early warning equipment on AWACS planes. Focusing on even the smallest sound wave just like a satellite antenna, this structure cannot be explained by the intelligence of an owl. Because the owl's ears were created asymmetrically (the right ear is higher), sounds reach the close ear 1/300,000 of a second earlier. This small time difference is enough for the owl to determine the exact location of the source of the sound. Through the 95,000 nerve cells in the simultaneous hearing center, the brain imagines a 3-D image of the prey. Due to the anatomy of it 14 neck vertebrae (humans and other mammals have seven vertebrae), the owl was given the capability of turning its head 270 degrees and determining the exact position of its prey. While flying towards the place

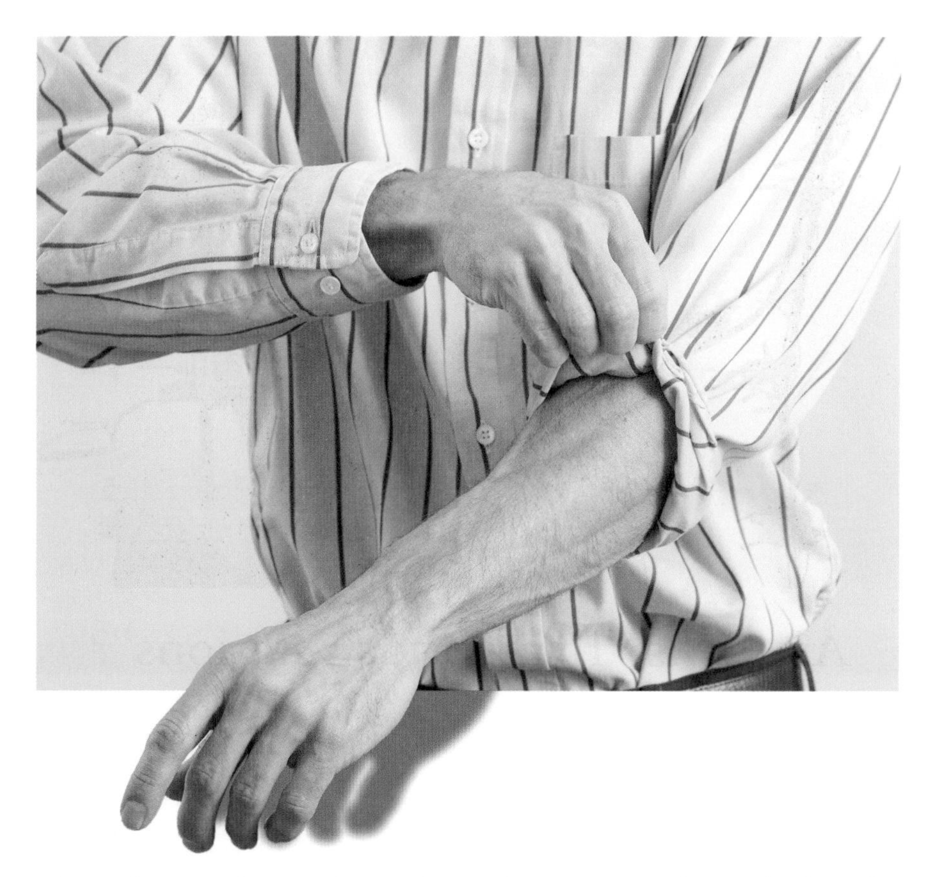

where the sound came from, the owl can constantly recalculate the position of the prey relative to its own position, even if the prey changes its place. As a result of this precise calculation, only three seconds passes between the moment the owl first heard the sound of the prey and the moment it makes its deadly attack.

What is tingling?

According to our posture position, when veins in our arms or legs tighten, the flow of blood in our veins is prevented. When pressure is removed, we feel stings at the edge of our legs till the blood flow is balanced and restored. This situation, that makes us feel as if thousands of ants were walking on our feet, is called tingling.

Can scratched CDs be fixed?

Most of the scratches on a CD emerge on the wax layer that protects the surface where the actual music is recorded. When this layer gets dirty or scratched, the laser light reading CD diverges and makes a mistake. The scratched part of the CD can be fixed by rubbing it slowly with a piece of extremely thin sandpaper and then waxing with a chemical substance. However, if the main layer is scratched, it is impossible to fix it.

Why do the nibs of some pencils write darker?

There are two substances called graphite and clay on pencil nibs. Graphite is a dark colored and soft substance which functions as lubricant in machines working at high temperatures. Clay is tougher than graphite and has a lighter color. Pencils that contain a high rate of graphite are softer and write darker, but those which have high rate of clay are tougher and write in a lighter color.

What do animals do when they get sick?

There are many examples of animals that treat themselves by means of the Divine guidance of God Almighty. Here are some of them: Lions take a little water and soil to their mouth and chew it when they are wounded. Then, they spit the mixture to ground and apply it on their wounds after kneading it little. In addition to sucking toxic substances on the wound, this mud also attracts the necessary substances for treatment towards the wounded area. Mammals generally lick their wounds. In this way, both the wound is cleaned and insects are kept away from the wounded area. Moreover, when a wounded tiger can't reach its wound, it rubs its spit with one of its front paws. When they can't reach their wounds, rainbow parrots make the treatment by rubbing their spit to the wound with the help of their mates. Wounded deer's and roes lie on mossy soils because there is a kind of antibiotic in mossy soils which treats wounds. While bears benefit from the curing aspect of honey by putting their foot into a beehive, bees recover by mixing their honey with an antibiotic which their body produces. Beavers are treated with a kind of jelly that is secreted from their body. When they get sick, cats and dogs eat grass and wolfs eat stinging nettle in pinches so that they can vomit. Also, wolfs have been observed to eat a plant called "gentian" when they get a snake bite.

Why do bees make their combs in the shape of hexagons?

Bees make their combs in the shape of hexagons in accordance with Divine inspiration. Because hexagon is a shape that can store the maximum amount of honey by using minimum material to build, it is the most beneficial and ideal form for making and storing honey. Besides, the resistance power of the hexagon-shaped comb is at a maximum. If combs were in circles, there would emerge pentagonal gaps between intervals. There wouldn't be any gaps left between triangle or quadrangle combs, but this time more material would be needed to build compared to the hexagon-shaped ones.

How can albatrosses fly for a long time without flapping?

Albatrosses that live most of their lives via oceans almost never land to the ground. They can ceaselessly fly for a long time and do not get tired. For these big sea birds, staying on air by opening their wings to the wind is enough for flying. They can fly for a long time in this way. They use warm air currents and wind for making their route in the sky. They make their miles-long way by passing from one air current to another. They fluctuate by zigzagging through the wind, wings wide open. Even though keeping their 3.5 meter wings open straight requires a certain amount of force, this is not hard for albatrosses because God Almighty has placed a special kind of lock system on their wing bones to keep their wings open. Thanks to this wonderful system, they can fly with a little energy without using muscle power, ceaselessly and tirelessly.

How do hibernating animals get nourished?

The process where many animals hide in suitable places and fall into a long sleep from the starting days of winter to warm days of spring is called as hibernation. The body activities of these animals slow down, and almost stop during hibernation period. Their body temperatures decrease to just about the temperature outside. Their heartbeats and respiration activities slow down very much and they fall into a deep sleep as if they were dead. Most of the hibernating mammals wake up one or two times along that period and eat their stored foods. Before hibernation, the animals feeling that winter has come, gain weight and stock plenty of fat in their bodies. This fat is used slowly to let the body work at a low but consistent pace during hibernation. Since they don't move, they don't need much energy. A good timing as it is, they finally awake at the end of winter just in time the stored fat is almost finished.

How do rubber erasers delete?

The fibers on the surface of a piece of paper break off during erasing because of the friction force between the eraser and the paper. Therefore, the graphite or ink that has filled the gaps between the fibers of paper is scraped along this process.

What kind of soil does tea plant like?

Tea plant grows in tropical and moist, showery mild areas, and it likes the particular kinds of soil that are very acidic and contain no lime. In addition to these conditions, a better quality is obtained at the areas higher than sea level. For the growth of tea plant, regular and continual rains are necessary, especially in early stages. While it is still green, tea plant reaches the length of 180 centimeters to be processed in the best way. Its length can reach up to 30 meters if it is left on its own. The Eastern Black Sea region in Turkey is very suitable for tea production in terms of soil and climate.

Why it is too difficult to fight with viruses?

The most interesting aspect of the smallest living creatures—viruses—is that they display both organic and inorganic characteristics in their nature. In their inorganic state, they are in a crystal form. When they enter a living creature's cell, their crystal form starts to display organic characteristics. Since they don't have organs like other creatures, they need another living being to activate their aliveness. In fact, everything depends on the Beautiful Names of God. Their body consists of only a single gene placed in a protein sheath. This protein sheath is the most important part of the virus because it can enter other cells through this sheath. The position of bacterium eating viruses gives the best example to clarify how a virus penetrates into the cell of an organism. Firstly, the virus clings to the bacterium with its tail part, and then it pierces the bacterium wall with its enzymes at the edge of the tail. In the last phase, the genetic codes of the virus penetrate inside the bacterium. In this way, the genetic codes of the virus capture the management of the invaded bacterium. Then, it starts to utilize the energy of that bacterium to meet its own energy need and multiplies the number of its own genetic codes. Through this invasion system, they increase their numbers. Finally, invading viruses multiply at such big amounts in bacterium that they free themselves totally by breaking bacterium into pieces. There are still some other cells to invade! Therefore, fighting with viruses is rather difficult.

What is regeneration?

Literally meaning renewal, regeneration could be defined as the completion of severed or injured pieces of an organism. The regeneration potential of living beings changes according to their needs. This potential has generally been granted to the animals which have comparatively many enemies and experience continual wounding and organ losses. Re-growing of severed tails of lizards and wigglers after a time can be given as a good example of this process. This potential is low in animals that can defend themselves, and very low in human beings who have been donated with reason and consciousness. God Almighty, who knows very well His creatures in the best way, has preserved all kinds of creatures by granting them the ability of regeneration in accordance with their particular needs.

Why should we lie on the right side of our bodies while sleeping?

While we lay our body on one side in sleep, one of our nostrils is blocked and the other one is opened according to the side we lay our body. And the respiration process is realized through the open nostril. In the case of laying on the right side, the right nostril is blocked and the left nostril is opened, and vice versa. If the respiration takes place through the left nostril, the activity of right brain hemisphere increases. Stimulating of the right brain hemisphere causes slowing down of heart beat, dropping in blood pressure and slowing down of stomach-intestine movements. Therefore, our heart is less tired, falling asleep becomes easier and this makes our resting more sufficient. Prophet Muhammad, peace and blessings be upon him, informed 1400 years ago that the best sleeping position is laying our body on the right side and pulling our feet towards the body, just like a baby in the mother's womb. Thus, the similarity between this body position with the fetus displays that this is an innate style of laying our body because while the baby is growing in his/her mother's womb, the muscles that are placed on his/her bones are in the original state, without contraction. After birth, all kinds of our movements are done by contracting these muscles. So, the best way of resting our muscles is putting our body to the state of our first creation period.

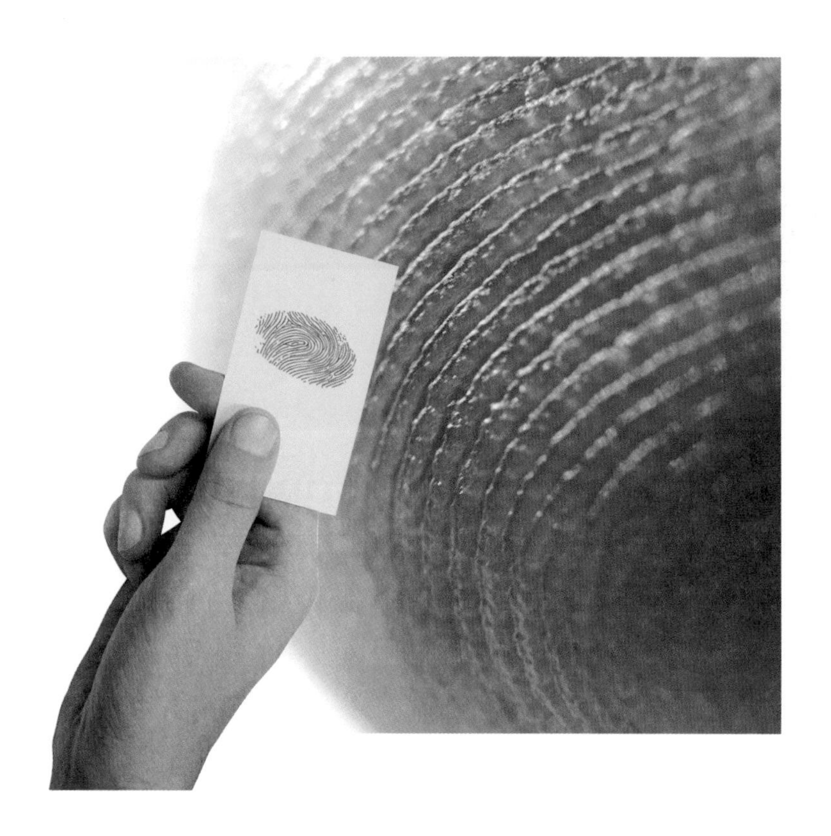

How does a fingerprint stay on the object we touch?

Sweat glands that are spread all over our skin were created with different density in every part of our body. There are many sweat glands on our fingertips, too. When we touch an object with our fingers, sweat coming out from the pores of sweat glands stays at the point we touch and causes our fingerprint patterns to be transferred to that surface.

Why do we stumble just after we stop circumvolving?

When we circumvolve and then suddenly stop, we can't adjust our body balance in a moment and stumble for a certain time. It is because of the fact that even though we stop circumvolving, the liquid in our balance organ (endolymph) that has been placed in our internal ear keeps moving for a short time. Our balance organ conveys messages about our body balance to the brain by assessing the movement of endolymph. For this reason, the continuation of endolymph's movement causes our brain to receive a message as if we were still turning. In the meantime, signals sent to the brain from the muscles and eyes inform the opposite, that we are not turning anymore. So, because of those simultaneous and different messages sent to our brain, we are not able to set up our body balance for a while. When the movement of endolymph stops and this message reaches to brain, everything returns to normal.

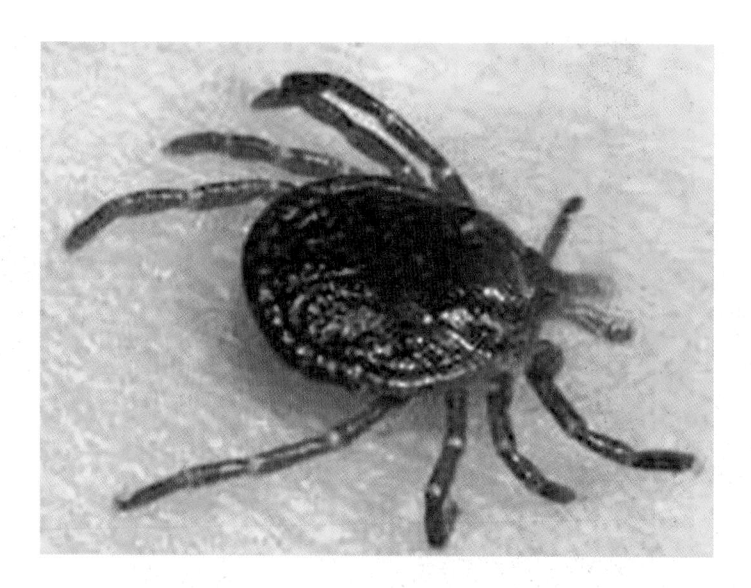

How shall we protect ourselves from acarids?

Acarids live on sucking the blood of living beings like human beings, sheep, cattle and dogs. There are many different kinds of acarids, but not all of them are harmful. However, particular kinds of them which live on humans and pets as a parasite can cause many diseases. The most harmful of these diseases is Crimean-Congo hemorrhagic fever. To keep being protected, it is essential to stay away from the places where they can intensively exist such as long grasses, lawns and bushes. In case of going to such places or picnic areas, all parts of our foot and legs should be covered very well, and all our body ought to be controlled after going back home. If an acarid has stacked on our body in spite of all these measures taken, we mustn't try to remove it by ourselves. Removing acarids from the body without killing, swatting and blasting is very important in order to prevent it from leaving harmful substances to the body. And this operation of course can only be done properly at a health institution.

What is adrenalin?

Adrenalin is a hormone which ingenerates in adrenal glands and mixes directly with blood as an increment substance. Taken even in a little amount, it increases the frequency of heart beats, enlarges the pupils, narrows down the veins and slows down movements of intestine.

What are the advantages of eating figs?

When we seek for the advantages of eating figs, on that God Almighty swears along with eating olive in the Holy Qur'an, we see this fruit is very rich in terms of vitamins and minerals. For example, one of these is the copper mineral which helps absorption of iron from intestines more. For this reason, it is very good to consume figs for adolescents and especially those who suffer from anemia. Fig is a very good source of calcium, too, because it contains more calcium than milk does. Besides, digestion of sugar in the fig that has no fat and cholesterol is easy and controlled. Herbal fibers in the fig present a critical service to our body. These fibers provide the controlled absorption of substance in the structure of the fruit in intestines. Therefore, both the sense of hunger decreases and the level of blood sugar and cholesterol are controlled. Especially, the fig eaten within an empty stomach in the mornings provides a particular cleaning of intestines by activating them. In addition to all these, there are some particular substances in the fig which have no nutritional value. As researches say, these substances have so unique characteristics that they can prevent cancer formation and cardiovascular diseases. That is, fig is actually both a nutrition and cure, bestowed upon us by the All-Merciful.

Why do droplets fallen on to superheated stove bounce?

When a droplet touches with the surface of the stove, the water layer under the droplet evaporates all of a sudden with the effect of the high heat. The droplet is flung up by the push of sudden volume increase taking place due to that sudden evaporation. When the droplet falls on the stove again, the same process repeats and the same bouncing happens again and again until the droplet evaporates completely. Meanwhile, the bouncing of the droplet presents an impressive spectacle. God Almighty has prescribed water with this ability and has inspired human beings the opportunity to produce energy by using steam power.

Does snow make the weather get cold?

Snow means that the weather is cold but the weather doesn't get cold due to snowing. On the contrary, snowing happens because the weather is cold, and snow surprisingly brings about a decrease in coldness. Here is the interesting explanation of the case: The required heat to melt 1 gram of a particular substance is called the melting heat of that substance. While transforming to water, ice takes a heat of 80 calorie for every gram. This is the melting heat of ice. While becoming ice, water gives out this melting heat. So, a heat of 80 calorie is given to the atmosphere during the freezing of every gram of water that transforms to a snow crystal. This case taken into consideration, the amount of the heat liberated to the atmosphere by 10 tons of snow is equal to the heat obtained by burning 100 kilograms of mine coal. This high amount of heat that water liberates while transforming to ice softens the coldness. Therefore, plants, animals and humans are being protected from the various damages of extreme cold. In spring, temperature of the atmosphere is decreased by 80 calorie heat taken for every gram from the atmosphere during the melting of snow. And so, damaging of developing plants from heat is being prevented.

How do security devices operating on entrance work?

Security doors warn officials by giving sound alarm in case a person passing through it carries a dense metal like a gun. Today, these doors are commonly used at the entrances of airports, hospitals, and shopping centers that are used by large amounts of people. The operating mechanism of these doors is that a weak magnetic field is made by a little electric current, and the circuit gives alarm when this magnetic field is cut by something.

Which fruits give happiness?

The level of happiness and liveliness is increased when people eat strawberries, bananas, grapes and oranges. For example, strawberry, a store of vitamin C, makes people gain extra youth and power, and decreases the high blood pressure by stimulating all the secretion glands in the body. Banana is a fruit that gives happiness even with its smell, and contains a rich amount of calcium and magnesium. It is especially good for people who feel tired and nervous. Possessing a good deal of the sugar in their nature, grapes are a very good nutrition for those people who work both physically and mentally. Finally, oranges make people gain extra dynamism. God's Beautiful Names function behind such veils.

How shall we consume black cumin?

The weakness of the immune system comes at top among the causes of getting sick. Black cumin seeds are so interesting that the Prophet Muhammad, peace and blessings be upon him, specifically ordains "This black particle is the cure for all diseases except death." It indeed has been created in such a specific nature that it contains particular substances to protect and strengthen our immune system. And it has been endowed to the service of humanity. We commonly consume this cure-source plant within a bakery diet. It is also recommended to take black cumin directly, or brew its tea and drink 2–3 glasses a day. It is very easy: Just pour some hot water on it, wait for 3–4 minutes, strain and drink. You can eat maximum 2 grams a day because it can cause diarrhea if it is consumed too much. Black cumin can also be consumed uncooked by mixing it with honey. However, since the husk of a black cumin seed can't be digested in our stomach in this situation, beneficial parts can't go to the necessary part of our body and the seed is thrown out within excreta. That is, if black cumin seeds are eaten with honey they should be pounded.

Do parrots understand what they say?

The most significant characteristics of parrots are imitating the sounds. They can utter words that they hear very often in exactly the same way, but, they don't understand the meaning of those words. They only articulate the sound they have heard before. Likewise, they can even imitate a doorbell and a phone ring. Therefore, if you keep a parrot at home, you can often presume that your door or phone rings.

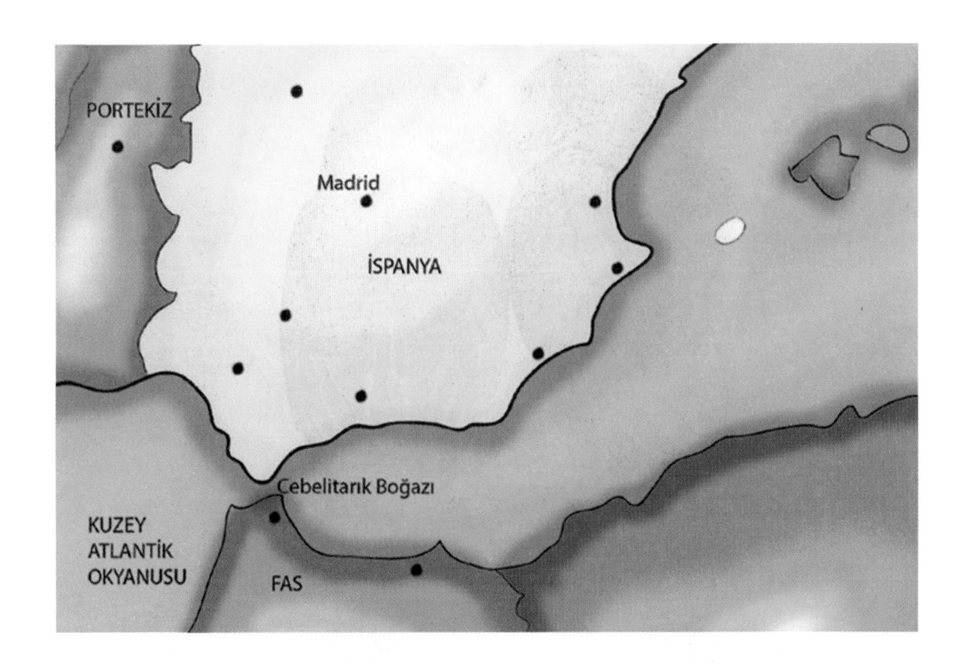

Which two seas are those that do not mix with each other?

There are many waves, strong flows and tides in the Mediterranean Sea and Atlantic Ocean. The water of the Mediterranean Sea meets with that of the Atlantic Ocean at Gibraltar. However, these two waters don't flow into each other because they have their own unique degrees of temperature, salinity and density. So, there is an invisible barrier between the two seas. God Almighty informs this miraculous situation in the Holy Qur'an as: "He has let flow forth the two large bodies of water, they meet together, (But) between them is a barrier, which they do not transgress (and so they do not merge)." (Ar-Rahman, 55:19–20)

How do leaves break off from trees?

Before trees shed their leaves, they start to suck all the nutritious substances in them. After some time, ethylene is produced in the cells of leaf blades (the straight and bright parts of leaves). Ethylene gas gradually spreads all over the leaf and when it reaches to leafstalk, it blows up the small cells in there. The leaves that can't stand this growing tension split off from the outer part of the stalk towards the inside. Rapid changes start happening around the expanding split and the cells immediately start to produce suberin. Due to the suberification, leaves completely split from the trunk. For this reason, leaves can't get the sap through conduction tubes and its bond with the holding point weakens gradually. Thus, in that final phase, even a light breeze can be strong enough to break off a leafstalk.

How does lotus keep itself so clean?

Lotus grows in a muddy and dirty habitat. The most significant quality of lotus is that its leaves always stay clean even though it grows in a dirty habitat. How does this miraculous event happen? When a little dust particle comes over the lotus, leaves are swayed and dirt is pushed to certain points. At the same time, this miraculous plant almost takes a bath by using rain drops. As rain drops are pushed towards the dirty points, dust is removed. This characteristic of lotus has given an idea to researchers for covering the outsides of buildings. Their aim is to build the surface of the outside of buildings in a way resembling lotus leaves so that the rainwater could clean the dirt as it flows.

What do Bower birds decorate their nests with?

Bower birds are noted for the way they decorate their nests. These big, gray Bower birds which only live in Australia decorate their nests with varied ornaments that they build in bushes. While some nests are decorated with 300–400 snail shells, some others are ornamented with white stones, glass and bone pieces, about 5000 in number.

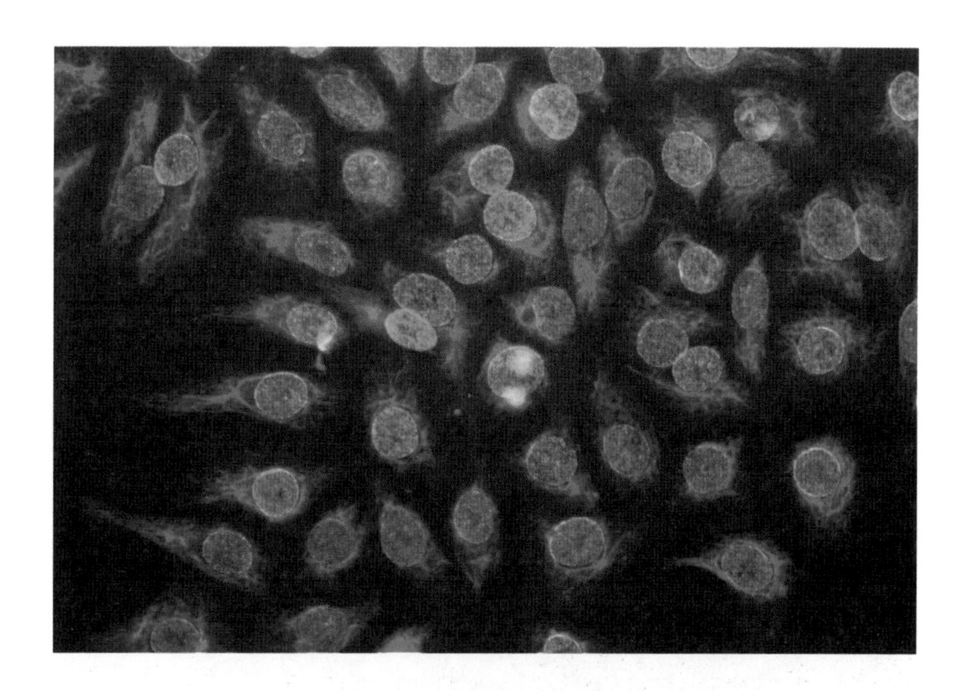

How do antibodies fight?

Sometimes enemy organisms can succeed in entering the body by overcoming obstacles like skin, respiratory and digestive systems. However, antibodies as powerful fighters of the immune system have been waiting for them. Antibodies are protein-structured weapons especially produced for foreign cells that somehow enter the body. These weapons are produced by "B" cells, one member of the army of immune system. Antibodies in charge of making invaders ineffective have two fundamental duties: First, attaching to the enemy cell that enters the body; second, damaging the biological structure of the enemy and getting totally rid of it. Antibodies exist in blood and the outer-cell liquid, and generally attach themselves to the bacteria or viruses that can cause diseases. They defuse the foreign molecules they have attached themselves to by marking them for fighter cells of body.

How does fan cool us?

There is another covering that surrounds our body just outside the skin. This moisture covering is originated by the steams of liquids which come out of our skin when we sweat. We can notice the existence of this invisible covering by condensation traces that come up when we touch cold objects such as windows, tables and glasses. This moisture covering which prevents our skin from drying, cracking and damaging, softens the sudden changes of temperature in the air surrounding us. No matter if the weather is very hot or cold, we generally feel it mild. However, a fast air current that occurs by factors such as winds, fans, or when we simply wave our hands toward our face hits our body and makes this covering get thinner. After that very moment, we start to feel the real temperature of the air surrounding us. Since the weather temperature is usually lower than that of our body, we feel cooler.

How do seals endure cold water?

Sea water, especially in depths, is very cold. Therefore, God Almighty creates seals living in cold water with a thick layer of fat covering their entire body. This layer under the skins of seals prevents them from losing their body heat quickly. Thanks to this creation, they can live in cold water easily. Another interesting quality of seals is that female seals give the richest and most nutritional milk to their babies. This rich milk helps young seals grow rapidly to cope with hard conditions they are raised in. What a beautiful sign of the All-Compassionate!

Why does the smoke of a barbecue always come toward us?

Because of the warming and dilatation of air layer just on top of the barbecue, its density decreases and it moves upward. The heat of the air around the barbecue is lower and its density is greater. This air layer moves toward the barbecue in order to fill up the space emptied by the air rising from the upside of the barbecue. But, this air current is prevented at the side of the barbecue where we stand because it hits us. As a result of this, the air currents coming from other sides of the barbecue direct the coming smoke toward where we stand.

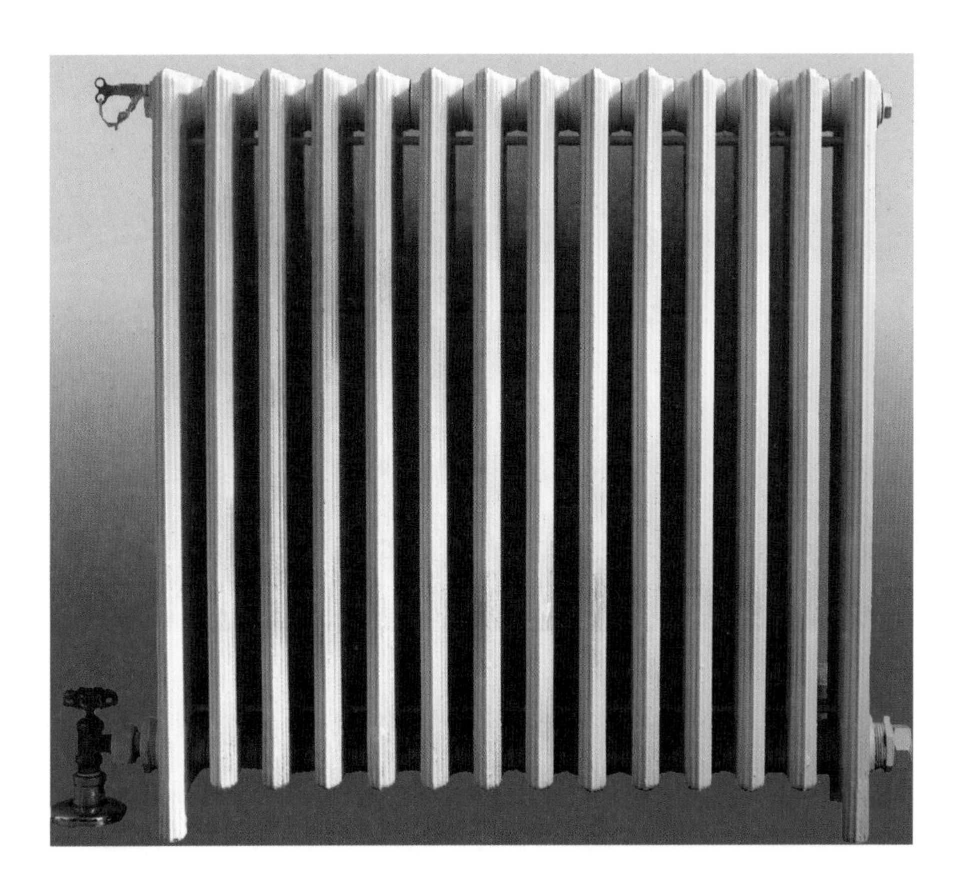

Why are heaters made with folds?

The hot water coming inside of the heater core firstly makes core walls get warm. Then, the core walls transfer the heat they have taken from the air surrounding them; and at the end, the place we are in gradually gets warmer. The larger the contacting area of the heater with the air, the more heat is transferred to the air. In this way, much more heat than the heat taken from the hot water coming to the heater is given to the air. For this reason, by making heaters with folds, the amount of the surface contacting with air is increased, and more heat transfer is realized.

Do Eskimos ever feel cold in their igloos?

Have you ever thought how Eskimos live in their igloos they made from snow molds? The walls of igloos are built with snow-made molds. These molds consist of snowflakes and air filled pores among these flakes. And it can be said that the larger part of snow molds consists of air-filled pores. The heat transmission potentiality of static air is lower than that of the solid substances. Normally it is expected that the heat transmission potentiality of that kind of porous objects is weak. Woolen clothes we wear in winter, roof tiles used in buildings and insulation materials can be given as examples of these kinds of porous structures. Through this system that obstructs the heat transfer from outside to inside and from inside to outside, even a little fire in these snow houses is warm enough to protect Eskimos against cold weather.

Why do curtains via the heaters get dirty more quickly?

The gases forming air are dilated and lose density when they heat up. For this reason, the heated air mass rises while leaving its place to the colder and denser air mass. Thus, an air current occurs from the floor of the room towards the heater, and then from there towards the ceiling. Namely, there becomes a circulation of air in the room. Curtains hanging via the heater filter the air that passes through them. The little foreign substances in the dirty air mass which can't be seen with the naked eye stay on the curtain and cause them to get dirty more quickly.

Why doesn't the stainless steel become rusty?

There is little difference between steel and iron. Raw iron is as soft as copper. By adding 2% carbon into it, an inconceivable degree of resistance, toughness and mechanical qualifications are obtained; and iron renders to steel after this operation. However, there is a weak point in steel like iron: rusting, in other words, oxidation. The level of humidity in the air plays an important role in rusting, too. One of the factors that increase the speed of rusting is salt. Because their atom sizes are very close to each other, some metals like chrome unite with oxygen very easily and rapidly. They make a very thin but very strong layer which has merely a thickness of a few atoms. Even if this layer is damaged, it takes place again. If chrome is added in steel in a certain proportion, the same event happens again, and steel doesn't get rusty after all. Due to this fact, be sure that there is 10–30% chrome in the stainless steel.

Do the batteries of radios run out faster when the volume is up?

Even though chargeable digital radios have become widespread today, we still meet with users of battery-powered radios. And battery life is important for these people while they use their radios. The loudness or lowness of volume affects battery life in battery-operated portable radios. The difference between the maximum and minimum levels of volume shortens the battery life. If the volume of radio is increased to the maximum level, the amount of the power taken from batteries increases 30%. This situation doesn't change for battery-operated devices such as radios, cassette players or walkmans.

Why don't we remember the events that happened to us before we were three years old?

To what age do you think people remember what they have experienced? Researchers have deduced that grown up people cannot remember what they lived until they were three years old. People cannot remember because it has been stated that human memory is arranged in the brain within the form of a recollection or story. Little children younger than three years old have the capability of talking correctly, understanding speech and keeping things in their memory. In spite of that, they can't shape events as a whole, and can't render them into stories. Due to this fact, human memory starts to record its experiences at the ages of 3 or 4, the earliest possible time.

Why do cloths shrink after washing?

Normally when a piece of cloth is washed, fibers on the cloth get swollen because of the wetness. In this situation, it is necessary for the cloth to stretch a little. But, because the pulling power generated by the abrasion in twists is more, the length of the cloth decreases, namely the cloth shrinks. After washing is completed, the swollen fibers of the cloth come to their original state. Still, the cloth can't reach to its original length because factors such as water, high heat, shaking of the cloth and soap facilitate the shrinking process. After a few times of washing, it is seen that the size of cloth reaches to a certain stability and there happens no shrinking in the following washings.

How do fireflies radiate light?

There is a light organ in the stomachs of fireflies. Two basic chemical substances taking part for producing light are released from the glands of this light organ. But, these chemical substances are not themselves enough to radiate light in a good way. For this reason, the respiratory organ of the insect ought to foster this particular area with oxygen during the process of radiation.

Why are most pencils made in a hexagonal shape?

In fact, the most suitable pencil type for holding is the square ones. But, it is quite hard to write with these kinds of pencils. To hold circular-formed pencils is easy but their production is rather costly compared to other types. So, the hexagonal pencils are the most suitable ones to use. Besides, their production costs less than the circular-shaped ones. And there is another aspect that will mainly interest naughty students: The hexagonal pencils are more suitable for playing games and rolling than the square-shaped ones. Also, if they fall down to ground during rolling they don't make much noise. Thus, they don't make naughty students be caught red-handed by teachers.

What is the reason why people have different voices?

There are many factors that affect the speech of people and articulation of voices from the mouth. So, it is almost impossible for two people to have the same voices. The most effective phenomenon in the articulation of human voice is the vocal cords. The length of the vocal cords determines the deepness and thinness of our voice. The longer the vocal cords, the thinner the voice comes out. Other organs helping the articulation of voice—apart from vocal cords—are our lips, teeth and tongues. If God Almighty had created only vocal cords but no other helping organs, just an incomprehensible bulk of voices would come out from our mouths. In addition to all of these, the character of a person, the flow and speed of the air, the formation of mouths and lips are also effective in speaking.

What does 24-carat gold mean?

"Carat" is a term that is used for displaying the pureness of gold. 24 carat gold is 100% pure gold which has not had any other metals mixed in it. Because the completely pure gold is very soft, it is generally mixed with copper or silver in order to make it more practical. Every carat is 1/24 of the whole gold. For example, if a bracelet is made from 18/24 gold and 6/24 from silver, this bracelet is classified as 18 carat gold. If gold is mixed with copper it is known as red gold; if it is mixed with silver it is called yellow gold and if it contains metals like nickel or platinum, it becomes white gold.

Why don't whales experience caisson disease?

Caisson disease is the greatest danger that a diver can experience. Divers don't face such a problem while going down from the water's surface to the bottom. But there would be a danger if a diver is going up to the water's surface from the depths suddenly and fast. In case someone goes up to the water's surface suddenly, the nitrogen gas dissolved in blood turns into bubbles. These bubbles emerging in veins harm the order of blood circulation that the veins of vital organs, such as brain and heart, are blocked and death risk ensues. This process is much like the carbon dioxide in a soda pop bottle that foams with bubbles when it is opened suddenly. As for whales, they have a very fatty, mucus-like special substance in the gaps in and around their lungs. This substance absorbs the nitrogen in the air. Because there is no free nitrogen left, the risk of bubbling in the veins is removed. Therefore, whales are protected from the risk of caisson disease. While exhaling, they spray this fatty substance in their breath tracks from the nostrils on their heads. Thus, neither the heart veins of whales get blocked nor their brains suffer from lack of oxygen. The All-Wise exhibits His amazing art to reasoning hearts...

Why do planes leave clouds behind them?

While forming clouds, water drops definitely need dust particles to hang on. At a height above ten thousand meters, one of the requirements to form a cloud is missing. By taking air from the front side, jet motors burn air with fuel. And after its function is completed, they leave the air out with a high pressure from the little exhaust behind. The water vapor that motors take with air becomes thicker in the motor and it is sprayed to the very cold air outside. In this way, the water in the form of vapor freezes directly, without turning into liquid as the breath we exhale becomes visible in cold weather. Besides, the function of dust particles is realized by the fuel particles coming out from the exhaust of the plane. So, three requirements to form a cloud are met, and long and thin clouds appear behind planes.

Why do we see blurry under the water?

In our daily life, the convex-shaped outer surface of our eye works as a lens. Without this lens, our eye can't focus the coming light on the retina layer behind our eyes. Light is refracted while passing through objects with varying density, e.g. passing from air to water or travelling in a prism. The density and convexity of our eyes are so wonderfully arranged that the coming light automatically focalizes in the retina after refraction. The speed of light in water is almost the same with its speed while passing our eyes. However, because the density of water is different, the light coming through water can't be refracted in our eye as the light coming from the air. The image can't focalize in the retina totally and we can't see objects clear under the water. If we put a glass between water and our eye and leave an air space behind it, the light passing from water to air and then coming to our eye is refracted normally and the image focalizes in retina clearly.

Why do stars blink at night?

We can see an object by means of the light reflecting from it. Because there is little light in the darkness of the night, many objects don't reflect their colors. So, we see all of the objects in a color very close to black. We notice stars and other celestial bodies (planets and moons) by their beams coming to us. However, there is a basic important difference between the lights coming from stars and other celestial bodies. Stars are individually sources of light, like the Sun. But, planets and moons reflect the light beams which they take from stars. Because of this fact, beams coming from stars are much brighter. The closest star to Earth is the Sun. But at nights, we can also see the stars whose beams come from a distance of millions of light-years. Why do these beams blink, then? The real cause of this blinking of stars is the disordered refraction of coming beams while they hit the moving air molecules in the Earth's atmosphere. Therefore, we see the star beams blinking though they actually come within smooth bundles as they come from the Sun.

Why does stinging nettle irritate our hands?

A special organic substance called formic acid has been endowed to stinging nettles so that they can protect themselves. They use this formic acid in self-defense against other living beings. Thanks to this instrument, its enemies can't come close to them. Formic acid is the same substance which hurts us in case ants bite us.

How much does our height keep increasing?

The amount of our tallness has been prescribed in the encoded information in our genes. But, genetics is not the only effective factor for our height. Our height can increase 5–10 cm. If a balanced diet program is followed throughout adolescence and sport is not neglected. The maximum probable tallness might be reached if fruit, vegetables and protein are consumed in sufficient amounts. Regular and satisfactory sleep is also another significant element.

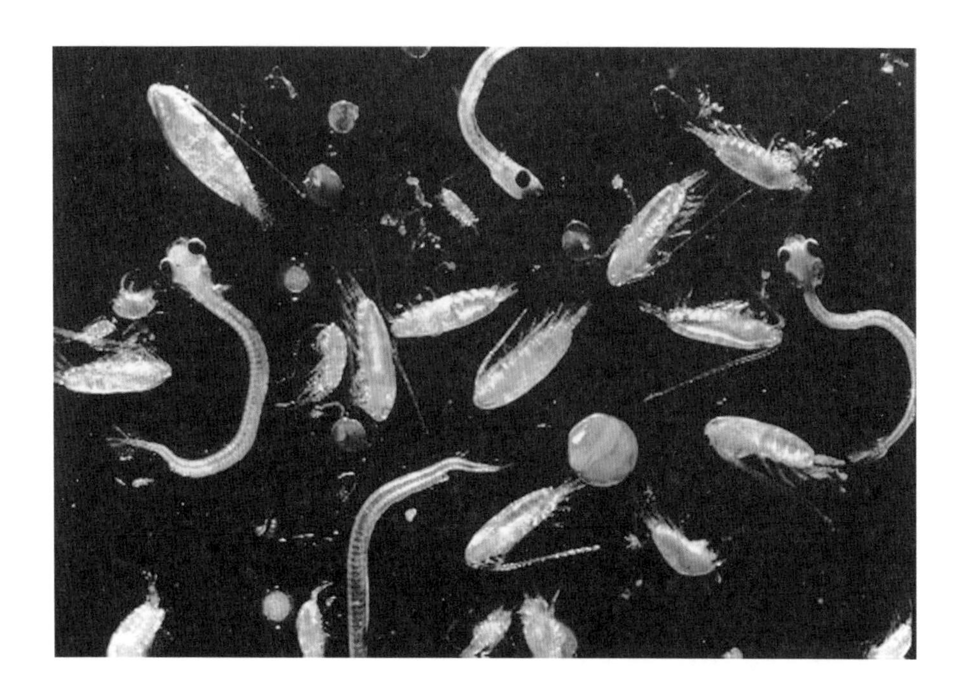

What is plankton?

Unicellular living beings which have been created compatible with the survival in oceans are called planktons. There are different types of planktons such as vegetal and animal. They are generally known as the nutrition source of whales. However, they have very important duties apart from this. One of them is filtering harmful sun lights. How do planktons do this indeed? Sulfured compounds generated in their bodies protect planktons from sea water. In case a plankton dies, sulfur mixes firstly to water and then to the atmosphere to frame the chemical structure of clouds. Commonly known, one of the duties of clouds is filtering the harmful lights coming to the Earth.

How do bearded vultures digest bones?

A bearded vulture, whose only food is bone, has quite a long stomach and intestine. So, it can swallow bones easily which are even 25 cm in length and 4 cm in diameter. Then, it digests them slowly. In order to enable it to swallow long and curved bones, its esophagus has been created flexible. Digestion of bones is realized by very irritant liquids generated in its stomach. For this reason, its stomach walls were covered by a lot of acid producing cells. Of course, these irritant liquids don't harm the bird itself.

Which insect has inspired human beings for helicopter production?

Wings of dragonfly—also called helicopter insect—are placed crosswise over its body and they are in a miraculous structure that can bear the body weight of it. This creation provides it to make sudden maneuvers and increase its speed, if needed. No matter how fast and to what direction it flies, dragonfly can suddenly stop and start to fly in the opposite direction. In a very short time, it can reach up to speeds changing from 50 km/h to 90 km/h. It is different from other insects with these qualifications that inspired human beings for helicopter production.

Why does our face blush when we feel warm?

The particular section of our brain, called Hypothalamus, always controls our body temperature like a thermostat. These controls are made in two different centers on the hypothalamus. One of these centers is designed to protect our body from temperature increase and the other for temperature fall. All changes in our body temperature are informed to these centers immediately by the receivers on our skin. These centers determine the activities according to incoming messages. If the information coming to the thermostat in the brain is about warming up, heat decreasing operations are started immediately. Firstly, a message for widening goes to blood veins under the skin. The aim is to transfer the heat inside firstly to the skin and then to the outside. When our veins widen, circulating blood transfers the heat it carries to the air easily. So, the reason for blushing in the face is those widening veins.

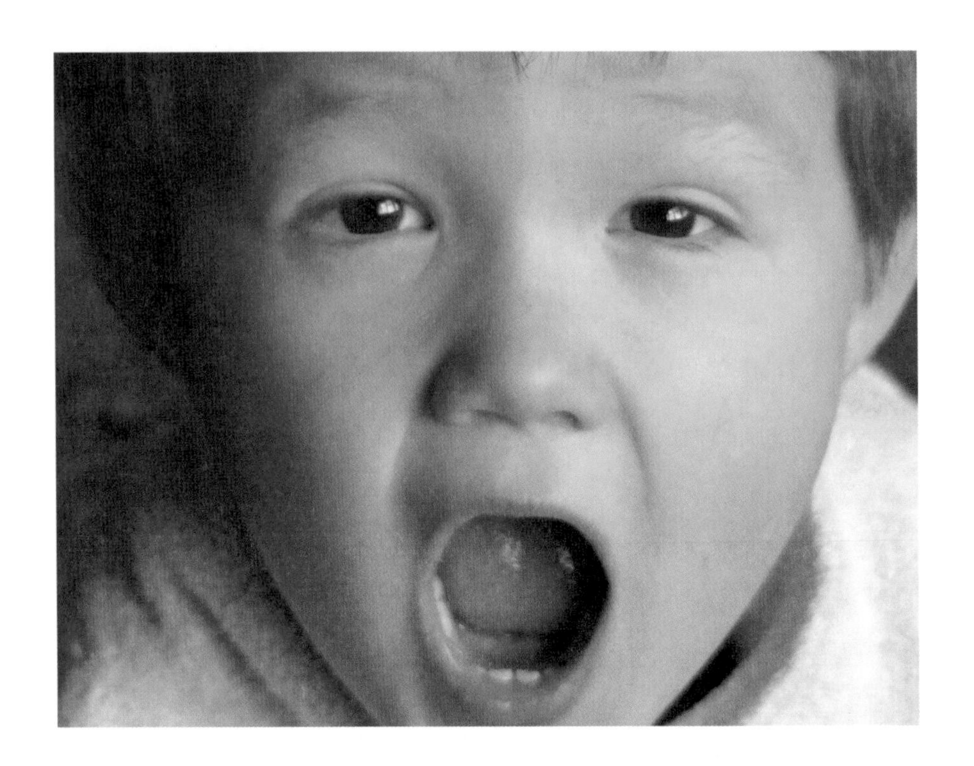

How is our voice generated?

While breathing, when the air we inhale reaches to our lungs, the oxygen inside the air mixes with the blood there. The carbon dioxide that comes out in the mean time comes back from the lungs and goes outside. While going out, it passes between the vocal cords which are placed in our throat. These cords, which look like a kind of curtain, stay open while we do not speak. They come together by the orders sent from the brain when we want to say something; and the gap between them is closed. So, the warm air coming back from the lungs passes over the vocal cords, not through them, before coming out from the mouth. As a result of this process, the vocal cords tremble like guitar cords by the touch of the plectrum, and our voice is heard.

What is an avalanche?

An avalanche is the falling of ice and snow masses toward a side of a mountain. After that huge amount of snow falls to mountains, the snow stratifies and becomes very heavy. This snow mass suddenly starts to slide by finding a suitable way and runs down toward the sides. Avalanches are mostly seen in spring. Snow starts melting as the weather gets warmer and sliding becomes easier. Earthquakes and sudden high-pitched sounds can also cause avalanches.

How do we know that the universe expands on and on?

Astronomers are able to measure which star and galaxies move and how much they move. Most of these star and galaxies move far away from us. It clearly means that the universe expands continuously, and becomes bigger than a moment before.

Which elements give light to fireworks?

Strontium element burns with red light, copper is with green, sodium is with yellow, barium is with green and magnesium is with bright white. Fireworks consist from the mixture of all these elements and this causes a multicolored burning.

Why are trees pruned?

If the top of a tree whose leaves are falling is cut approximately two meters, the same part grows up again in a renewed condition, and the tree rises better this time. This is called pruning. Pruning is both useful for the tree and we can get the needed material from the tree at the same time. Branches of non-pruned trees don't grow as well as the pruned ones.

What is a cramp?

When a lot of lactic acid is secreted in muscles, this situation causes strong and painful hardening in muscles. This is called a cramp. Cramp occurs after sudden or excessive using of muscles we operate rather less, or a sudden standing up while sitting in an unsuitable and uncomfortable position. What we ought to do in case of a cramp is simple: opening and stretching movements in a slow pace and massaging the affected area.

Why do balloons blow up when they are pressed?

When a balloon is pressed, the volume of the gas inside it decreases greatly. Since the volume and the pressure of the gases are in inverse proportion, the pressure of the gas increases a lot while its volume goes down. The balloon blows up with the effect of this increased pressure. In 1662, Robert Boyle studied the attitudes of substances in the gas form.

How do crystals come into existence?

Crystals can be solid and in many other forms in nature. A lot of solid substances, almost all metals and minerals, exist in the form of crystal. We can observe crystallization in a sugar solution. If we add sugar in water, sugar is dissolved in the water and a sugar-water mixture emerges. Then, if we boil this solution up to its boiling point, the water starts to evaporate. The solution whose water gradually decreases contains more sugar in its new form compared to before. Finally, the water evaporates totally and the water and the sugar separate from one another. As a result of this, the sugar crystallizes, too.

How do mirrors reflect images?

Every surface reflects light including the pages of this book which you are looking at now. However, because they are very wavy, many surfaces spread the light to different points and it is scattered very much. But, because mirrors reflect the light parallel and as a whole, a very bright and clear image is obtained.

When was the first photograph taken?

The first known photograph was taken by French scientist Joseph Niépce in 1826. This first system used to consist of a lean and tin mixture plate which is covered by asphalt and a window that displays the image. 8 hours were needed to take one pose of photograph. Then, new styles of taking photographs were developed in 1830s and 1840s. Those photographs, known as photographs taken on to silver, were done and used by French and English people. In 1888, an American, George Eastman invented Kodak machine which contains film sheets.

How do chameleons catch their hunts?

Chameleons are a kind of lizard which live on trees and have been created in such a particular way that they can transform their skin color into the colors around them. They can hide themselves from enemies by changing their colors when they get angry or excited. They can turn even into black with anger. While chameleon is hunting, firstly it besieges around its hunt and stays calm. At this time, the eyes of a chameleon take photographs of the hunt functioning independently. Then, the chameleon attacks the hunt suddenly with its tongue. The hunt doesn't have any chance to escape.

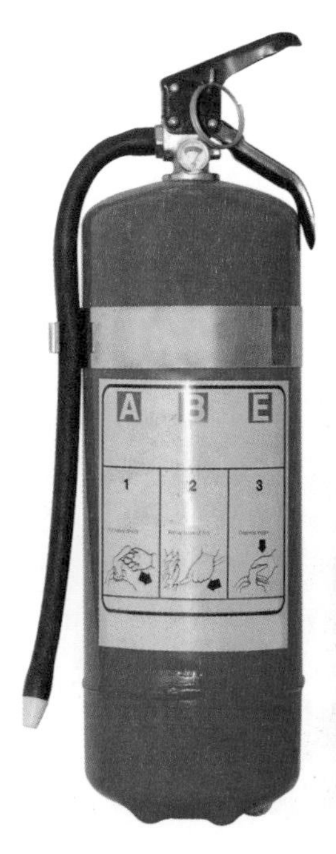

Why is carbon dioxide used for extinguishing fire?

Oxygen is needed for any kind of burning. Carbon dioxide is a heavier gas than oxygen and air. When we spray carbon dioxide to fire, it makes a layer between the flame and the air. The contact of the flame with air is cut through this layer. The flame that can't reach the oxygen needed for burning can't continue to burn. We are rescued from fire in this way. The discovery of this qualification of carbon dioxide has opened the way to use it in fire extinguisher tubes. Besides its fire extinguishing qualities, it is preferred since it is liquefied and filled into tubes easily.

Why is olive a miraculous nutrition?

Raisers of olive trees must be as patient as olive trees. Their lives can expand up to 1000 years. Olive trees that start to bear their first fruits after 7–8 years, give their maturity fruits at the age of 35. Besides its unknown qualities, the known benefits of olive are as follows: It prevents embolism; contains cancer preventing substances; makes digestion easier; provides a younger skin appearance; enables our hair to shine by thickening it, provides well operation of intestines by preventing constipation; and takes a big role in putting blood pressure under control.

Why do birds migrate?

Ever year, birds depart to different regions according to weather conditions and food opportunities. In fact the saying "they are sent" is much more correct. The Creator, God Almighty knows the needs of all creation and so He placed this information into the body of birds. Surely, it may not be thought that birds contrive by "reason" to migrate to warmer regions in winters. Many bird species like water birds, singing birds and sea birds lead their lives by migrating to various regions according to summer and winter conditions.

Why does iron rust?

When an unpainted iron stays in a humid place for long time, brown dust covers it. This situation is called rusting or oxidation. Well, how does this oxidation take place which causes decaying of a hard metal like iron? Oxidation can be summarized shortly as it is "the combination of iron with oxygen and the production of a new compound." If the place iron stays is very humid, the rusting process accelerates. For this reason, metals like iron are painted so that their contact with air and water is cut, and rusting is prevented.

Which fish is the strongest among the fish that generate high voltage electricity in their bodies?

It is the electrical snakefish. Electric organ of snakefish is its whole body and it consists of tens of thousands of electric cells. These cells are placed one after another as plaques on the belly of the fish. A strong electric current is obtained if the fish empties the total charge of them at the same time. The voltage of this electricity generated is 500 volt at average. The snakefish that generate even 650 volt electricity have been observed. This electric charge with 2 amperes current value is even stronger than the amount that is needed for operating a television. Electric fish use this power while hunting or defending themselves. They daze their hunts with this electric current and then eat them. Sometimes they facilitate electricity to frighten their enemies.

Is there a plant eating insect?

Plants such as sundew and Venus flytrap are plant eating insects. These plants survive in weak, poor and unproductive soils. The soil of the regions they live don't supply enough mineral for their nourishment. For this reason, this kind of plants has been created in a particular nature that they can make insects fall into their traps. Leaves of sundew are sticky and stingy. Venus flytrap plant has a wonderful ability of catching insects. By means of their creational traps, insects stick to these plants. These plants transform stuck insects into nutrition for themselves by melting them with acidic chemical substances in their bodies.

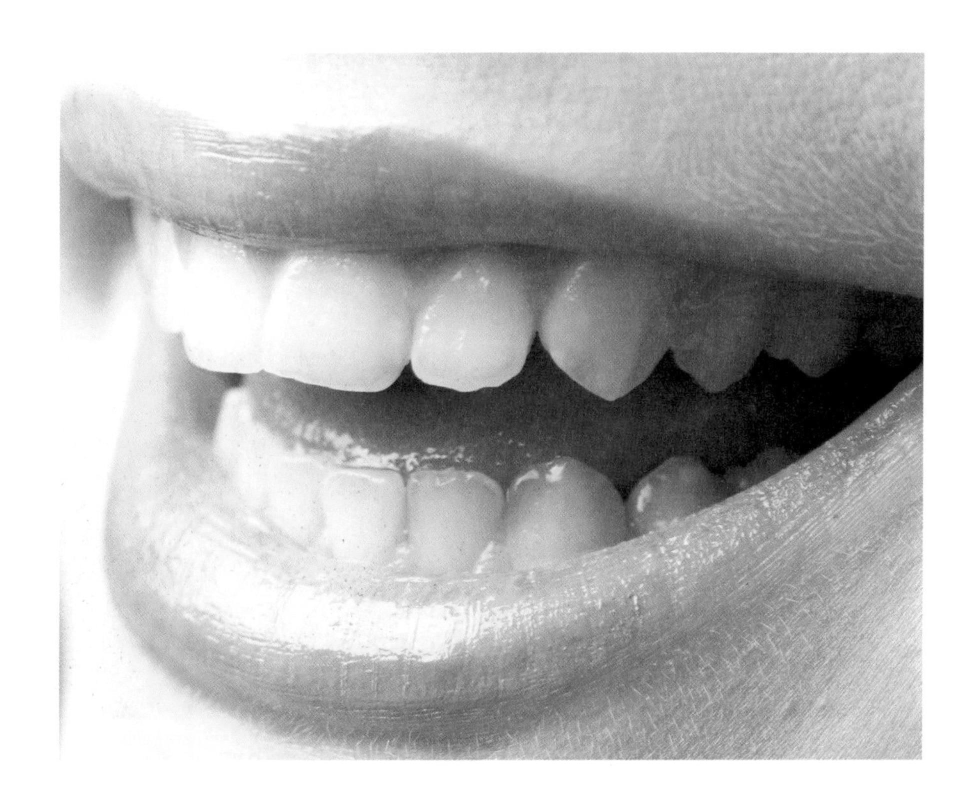

Why are the shapes of our teeth different?

The shapes of our teeth are different from each other because each of them has a different function. The shapes of front incisors are like an incisory device. These teeth have been given to us for cutting and gnawing. The canine teeth are next to the incisors. The function of these teeth is smashing of the nutrients that have been cut off by incisors. The molar teeth are placed at the very back of our mouth and they work for grinding nutrients.

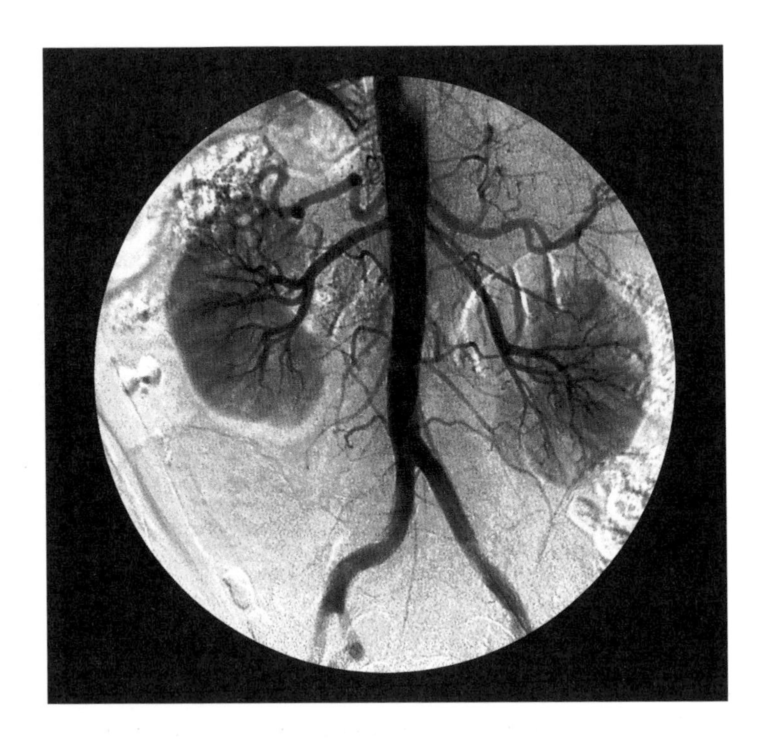

How does a kidney machine work?

The kidney machines realize the process of filtering blood and this process is called dialysis. While connecting people to this machine whose kidneys don't work as they should, the performance of our kidneys is tried to be obtained. A tube is placed to the arteries of the patient and this tube carries the blood in the veins to the machine. Then, this blood moves forward through a device which is called as cellophane. Through this system, the machine does the process of filtering which the patient's own kidneys can't do. The machine gives back beneficial substances to blood and throws out useless ones by filtering. Then, the processed blood comes back to the body of the patient. During this process, the patient's blood should pass through the machine almost 20 or more times. When we look at the operating system of this machine, we can see and wonder how our kidneys can do a vital process in one drive, by obeying the Divine command.

Why do computers make noise while operating?

A computer consists of particular parts such as a monitor, case, keyboard and mouse. The larger amount of needed electric energy for a computer is used in circuits in the case. Since the usage of electric energy causes warming up in circuits, substances suitable to burning can easily catch fire. In order to prevent that kind of accidents, a fan which consists of a little turning fan blowing while computer is on is attached to a side of the case opening to the outside. That fan enables the transfer of emerging heat to the air circulating among the circuits while providing continuous air entry from the outside to the inside of case. In this way, dangerous warming ups are prevented. The sound that comes out while computer is on belongs to this fan.

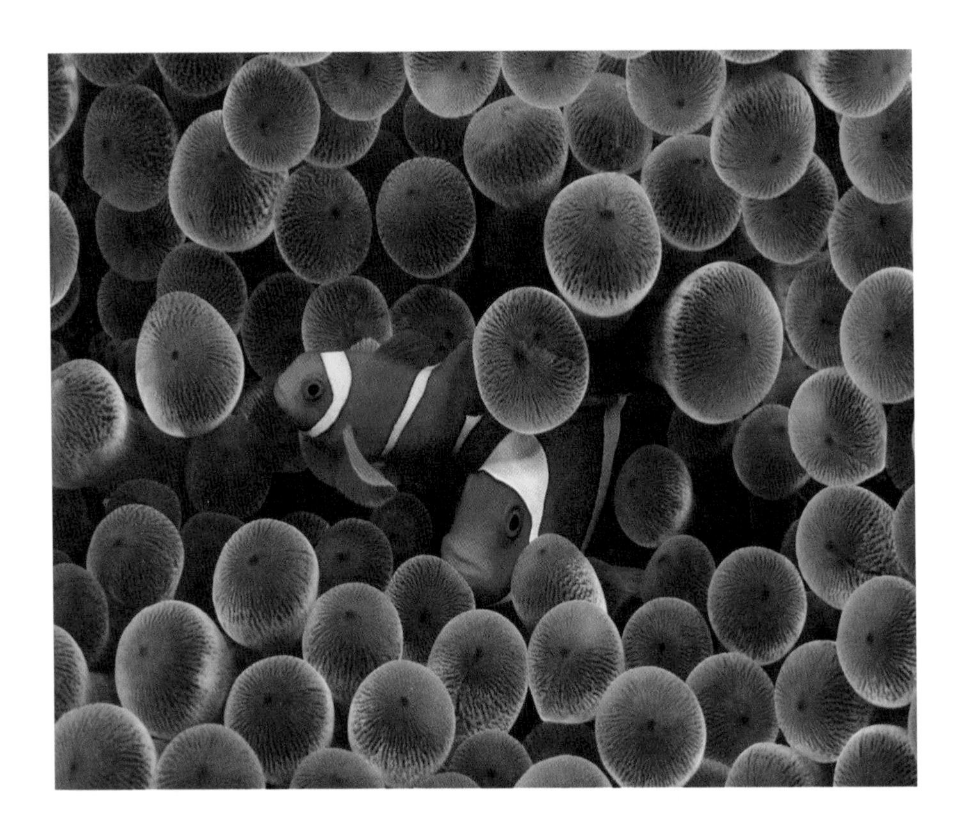

How do clown fish and sea anemone cooperate?

Cooperation of clown fish with sea anemone is worth watching. If a clown fish finds a bigger nutrient for its teeth, it brings it to the sea anemone and asks for help. Sea anemones cut the nutrient into pieces for the clown fish. Then the clown fish cleans the upside of the sea anemone. By this Divine guidance, while one of the partners is nourished the other one is cleaned at the same time. One of the innumerable facts showing that life is not a struggle, but cooperation…

Why do we add salt to meals?

Salt is a compound which consists of sodium and chlorine elements. Sodium in the salt is necessary for absorption of simple sugars which are the basic units of carbohydrates and amino acids, the basic units of proteins. Therefore, if the salt isn't added to meals, carbohydrates and proteins which are essential nutrients can't pass into the blood and be thrown out from intestines without absorption; that is, essential nutrients may be wasted. Thus, salt that seemingly makes our meals delicious is actually charged with enabling nutrients to pass into the blood. In order to encourage people to take salt with meals, which has an essential role for the health of body, the All-Merciful has loaded salt with the charge of adding taste and flavor to our meals as well.

Why do we generally feel thirsty after meals?

When we drink water in times we are hungry or when there is no nutrient in intestines, the larger amount of this water can't pass into the blood. Probably, we don't need to drink water when our stomach or intestines are empty for not wasting it in the stomach. Even if we still do, we can't drink much. The wisdom behind the need of drinking water generally after meals is that the water drunk after meals both makes digestion in stomach and intestines get easier and the nutrients pass into blood.

Why should we smile?

Smiling is a movement which relaxes our body and increases our resistance against diseases as it refreshes some particular secretions in our body. First of all, being able to smile is a positive sense. It is known that positive senses have a positive effect on healing and strengthen the feeling of hope in human beings. Besides, it is observed that people with positive senses are more successful in their relationships and lives. Positive senses and behaviors are like a key in human relations. A sincere smile may open even the doors of a person's heart to us. Besides, "smiling is a charity," as the Prophet Muhammad, peace and blessings be upon him, ordained. Interestingly, only 17 face muscles begin to act for a smile whereas making a sulky face causes more face muscles to operate and get tired due to the consumption of more energy.

How does carrot affect eyesight quality?

The beta-carotene substance in carrots conduces to protection of eyesight health, especially night vision ability. After transforming into vitamin A in the liver, beta-carotene is carried to the retina layer of eye for being converted to rhodopsin which is an essential pigment necessary for a good night vision. Sight in poor-lightened environments is possible by means of this pigment. Therefore, a decrease in night vision ability signifies vitamin A deficiency. God Almighty has charged the antioxidant in beta-carotene to be a protector against the sight diseases and cataract which develops in old ages.

How do horses see?

Horses are endowed with an ability of using eyes independently from each other. In other words, both individual eyes of horses can see different objects independently at the same time. This advantage provides horses seeing from the sides, front and back. Two eyes are placed on two sides of their head and they can see around with an angle of 160–170 degree. Therefore horses see a wider area than people as they have almost totally 320–340 degree sight angle. This situation enables horses to see almost everything around them, except the back of its tail while keeping its head straight. When horses want to see an object clearly, they turn their face to that object and they can focus to the object from different distances. Turning its head down or up is enough for this focusing. In this way, the image of object is dropped clearly over the retina by focusing according to the distance of the object. Through this perfect ability that has been given to horses by God Almighty, horses can manage the distance of a stick and the jumping point easily.

How are ceramic tools made?

The materials such as pots and pans which are made from a certain kind of soil transformed to dough with water and toughened by firing in ovens are called ceramic tools. Plus, the art of making these tools also has the same title. Clays are the essential raw materials of ceramic works. Dough, which is made from clays, is shaped by turning in lathe or pouring to particular molds. After the dough-shapes have been prepared in these ways, they are dried for a while and fired in the oven. They are fired one more time after being covered by glaze or varnish, in accordance with the kind of work. It is possible to make ceramics in desired shapes and decorations on them. For this, desired ornaments and decorations are applied either just after the first firing or after process of glazing and varnishing.

Why does the sky thunder?

Thunder is the noise we hear after lightning flashes. The very strong electric current which causes the occurrence of lightning warms up the air intensely in a short time before lightning flashes. As a result of this warming, a sudden enlargement happens in air molecules. Enlarging air starts flowing quickly towards the area where the cold air resides. As a result of this movement of the enlarged air, thunder takes place.

Does sweat have a particular odor?

God Almighty has placed in total 2.5 million sweat glands on our body, almost 100 units in every centimeter square. Sweating is a balancing activity which takes place to make the body temperature remain at the desired interval and keep the body comfortable. Some of our body mechanisms are put into function for balancing the body temperature when we enter into a hot place. And our body temperature is balanced with a system that works as a thermostat. Sweat is normally scentless, but it gains particular odor depending on the combination of sebaceous gland secretions and bacteria in our body. People generally complain about sweat because of its odor; and they even try to prevent sweating. But, cosmetic products that are applied to the underarm for preventing sweat cause the closure of sebaceous gland pores. And this leads to some of the harmful substances which ought to be removed from our body to remain inside and infest it. The best way to get rid of sweat odor is having a bath often. Besides, when we don't take a bath after repeated sweating, toxic substances which are thrown out by sweat before can be absorbed back. Since sweating is a defense mechanism, preventing sweating increases especially the risk of sunstroke in summer.

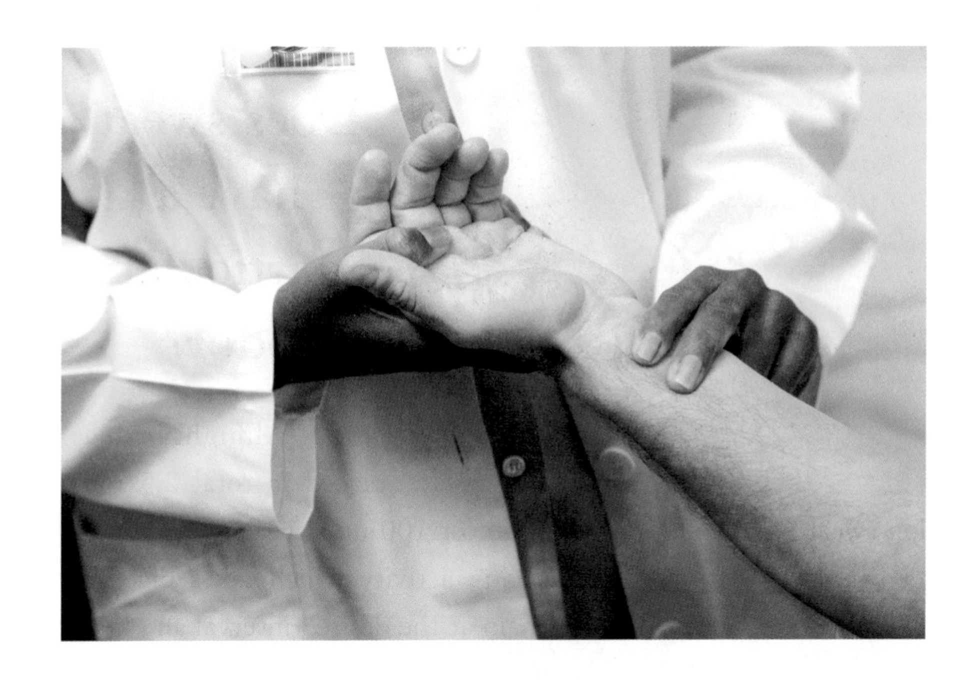

What is pulse?

Pulse reflects how many times the heart contracts in a minute; namely, it is the speed of heart. With each contraction, our heart throws some amount of blood to the inside of arteries. Our Lord Almighty has endowed our veins with the ability of flexing. With the coming of blood, an expanding takes place in our arteries, and then they want to relapse. This expanding is felt as pulse wave in the points where our veins are close to the skin such as writs, inside of our elbows, groins, temples and ankles. Pulse gives information both about the speed of our heart and whether our heart operates systematically or not. For healthy people relaxing, pulse should be 60–100 per minute, 70 in average.

Why can't we see around us for a while when we enter into a dark place?

Adaptation of our eyes to a new situation, as passing from darkness to light or from light to darkness, is related with the cone and stem cells in eyes. Cone cells are on duty at light places, stem cells are on duty at dark places. When we enter a dark place from a light place, firstly we see all around as completely dark. After a while we can start to perceive the things around. Because of the sudden decrease of light, the duty of cone cells operating in light shall be transferred to stem cells which function in darkness. And this shift needs a short period of time. After a short while, everywhere is completely dark for us. It is just after stem cells step in that our eyes get used to see in darkness. Just the opposite, everything is very bright for us when we come out from a dark place to light. This time, cone cells become active and our sight becomes normal after a short while.

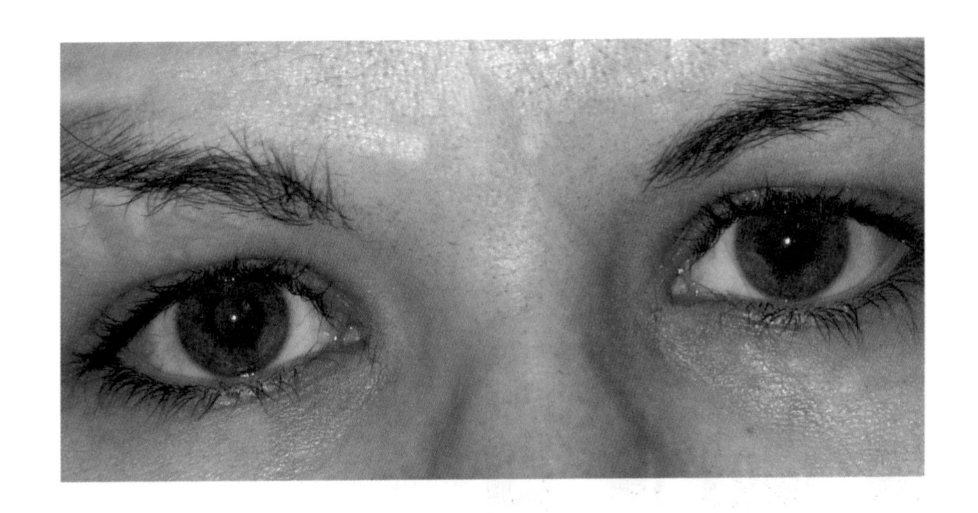

Why are our eyes red in some photographs?

Our eye which has been created in a perfect form with all its aspects consists of some particular layers. There are many blood veins between the retina and sclera, the white part of the eye. The reason of red eyes seen in some photographs is related with the amount of light coming to this layer. Red eyes are seen generally in the photographs which are taken in dim light. Pupil is the responsible area for arranging the entering light to the inside of our eye. In the case of low light, our pupil enlarges in order to let more light into our eye. If the flash of camera is lit at that moment, unnecessarily more light enters into our eye. The layer which has dense blood veins reflects the coming light back and so our eyes become red in photographs. This situation is prevented in the cameras which pops a separate light before the flash. By means of the warning of the popping light before, our pupil gets smaller to let less light into our eye. Therefore, when the actual flash is lighted, no more than necessary light reaches to our eye.

Sources

- *107 Kimya Öyküsü*, L. Vlasov, D. Trifonov, Ankara: TÜBİTAK, 1998
- *Bilim ve Teknik*
- *Bilim Çocuk*
- *The Fountain*
- *Gündelik Bilmeceler*, Partha Ghose, Dipankar Home, Ankara: TÜBİTAK, 2002
- *Hayvanlar Ansiklopedisi*
- *My Big Question and Answer Book*, London: Kingfisher, 1999
- *National Geographic*
- *Seçilmiş Gezegen*, Aslı Kaplan, İstanbul: Muştu, 2008
- *Sızıntı*
- *Tabiatta Mühendislik*, M. Sami Polatöz, İstanbul: Kaynak, 2003
- *Zafer*

Web Sites

- www.biltek.tubitak.gov.tr
- www.biltek.tubitak.gov.tr/cocuk
- www.fountainmagazine.com
- www.kimyaokulu.com
- www.nix.nasa.gov
- www.nsf.gov
- www.sizinti.com.tr
- www.zaferdergisi.com